KICKSTARTERS

101 ingenious intros to
just about any Bible lesson

KICKSTARTERS

101 ingenious intros to
just about any Bible lesson

Rick Bundschuh & Tom Finley

ZondervanPublishingHouse

Grand Rapids, Michigan

A Division of HarperCollinsPublishers

Kickstarters: 101 ingenious intros to just about any Bible lesson

© 1996 by Youth Specialties, Inc.

Youth Specialties Books, 1224 Greenfield Dr., El Cajon, CA 92021, are published by
Zondervan Publishing House, 5300 Patterson Ave. S.E., Grand Rapids, MI 49530.

Library of Congress Cataloging-in-Publication Data

Bundschuh, Rick, 1951-
    Kickstarters: 101 ingenious intros for just about any Bible lesson / Rick
Bundschuh, and Tom Finley
        p. cm
    Includes index.
    ISBN 0-310-21527-7
    1. Church group work with youth. 1. Finley, Tom, 1951-   Title.
BV4445.B774 1996
268'.433–dc21   96-46631
                                                 CIP

Unless otherwise indicated, all Scripture quotations are taken from the *Holy Bible:
New International Version (North American Edition)*. Copyright © 1973, 1978, 1984 by
International Bible Society. Used by permission of Zondervan Publishing House.

Edited by Lory Floyd and Tim McLaughlin
Design and illustration by Michael Kern
Production by Intel Design

Printed in the United States of America

97 98 99 00/ /4 3 2

Contents by topic

Contents by topic (continued)

Contents in alphabetical order

INTRODUCTION

- All the way to church in their mother's minivan, Ralph and Thelma argued; little wonder they entered the youth room with frowns and snarls.

- Myron is attending the meeting under duress—his mom threatened to burn his sports card collection unless he got moving that morning and came to church.

- Zelda is madly in love. She thinks that Butch really likes her because she caught him staring at her during school lunch. Actually, she had bird droppings on her shoulder—but hey, it's a start. She can't wait to blab the exciting gossip.

Into the meeting room they trudge. A couple dozen kids with a couple dozen distractions floating around their heads. None of them are eager to hear the glad gospel tidings and godly nuggets you've studied so hard to bring to them.

Enter *Kickstarters*.

A Kickstarter is an opener for your Bible lesson, not the lesson itself. A Kickstarter grabs the attention of all of those focused-on-other-things minds and gets them thinking along the same track. In this book are 101 such Kickstarters, on more than 70 topics that matter to teenagers today.

Want to teach a lesson on loving others? Check out "Velcro Man" (kids throw sticky Ping-Pong balls at a Velcro-covered volunteer), or a "Ten Years and Counting," a milder lesson opener about how your kids picture themselves ten years down the road (the perfect lead-in to a discussion about the future).

Some of these Kickstarters get a laugh, some of them provoke serious thought—but they're all workable. Whatever your tastes, whatever the style of your youth group, you'll find a year's worth and more of ways to get your kids immediately immersed in your subject.

How to Use *Kickstarters*

First, the *formal* way to use *Kickstarters*. Say you've decided to teach your students the evidence for God's existence (hey, why mess with sex and dating when you can go right to ontology?). Check the table of contents on page 5, where you'll find the title of each Kickstarter listed under its topic (topics are arranged alphabetically). And right there under the topic GOD, EXISTENCE OF, you'll find the Kickstarter "World's Heaviest Baby"—and now your lesson can start with a bang.

The *informal* way to use *Kickstarters*—or if your topic isn't listed—is to just skim through the book until you find a Kickstarter whose activity can be reworked to suit your need. You'll notice as you flip through the book that in the upper corner of each page is the topic or topics that Kickstarter deals with. You'll find plenty of inspiration to unlock your own creativity.

Although it's up to you to create your actual lesson that follows the Kickstarter intro, each Kickstarter suggests what kind of a lesson can follow, or suggests a segue, or connection, that eases your group from the Kickstarter into the lesson itself. And if our suggestions don't work for you, tweak the tone or the doctrinal slant to make it a fit for your group.

Now off to attention-getting, roaring starts to your Bible studies!

The Shirt Off My Back

Provide large white T-shirts for your students (or have them bring their own). You'll also need a bunch of fabric paint in squeeze bottles. Have each student put on a T-shirt. Hand out the paints, then stand the group in a circle, kids facing each other's backs, so the kids can work on the back of the person in front of them.

At the signal ask each student to paint on the shirt a word about the wearer that is uplifting, affirming, humorous, or in any other way positive. Painters shouldn't tell the wearers what word they're painting. After a minute or two, rotate so that everyone is painting on someone new.

In a small group kids can write *two or three words* on the person in front of them.

CONNECTION

Use this Kickstarter to introduce a lesson about the importance of speaking affirming or uplifting words to each other. A lesson on how Christ affirmed his disciples would be particularly appropriate, or perhaps one on how Christians—the body of Christ—can care for and love each other.

Stamp of Approval

Guide your students into a Bible study highlighting our need to affirm and love each other.

Locate enough rubber stamps so that each student has one. It doesn't matter what kind of imprint the stamp makes. Have a few stamp pads of various colors. Then arrange for one student—probably a male—to come to the meeting wearing his bathing suit.

Stand your bathing-suit-clad kid in the middle of the room—then give everyone the go-ahead to "leave their mark" on him. In mere minutes he'll look like a carnival Tatoo Man. Leave him in his bathing suit for the whole lesson.

CONNECTION

All of us leave an impression on those around us, whether for good or for bad. Tell your students:

Notice how well covered with your marks our pal is. In everyday life each one of us leaves our mark, our impression, our imprint on those around us—words that either affirm or ridicule someone, behavior that either helps or mocks someone. Let's take a moment and consider some ideas from God's Word about how we might better put the stamp of his love on one another.

My Favorite Church

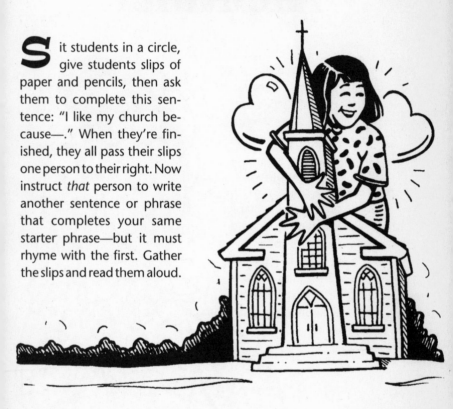

Sit students in a circle, give students slips of paper and pencils, then ask them to complete this sentence: "I like my church because—." When they're finished, they all pass their slips one person to their right. Now instruct *that* person to write another sentence or phrase that completes your same starter phrase—but it must rhyme with the first. Gather the slips and read them aloud.

CONNECTION

The phrases will range from silly to serious, but they're a fun way to begin a study about the church.

The Ruler

Why believe the Bible over other holy books? Because it has the authority of God's truth behind it. This Kickstarter centers your group's attention on the Bible's authority.

Have students guess the length of various objects in the room—a wall, door, window, table, anything. Record these guesses on your whiteboard or chalkboard.

When everyone has guessed, use a tape measure to find the accurate lengths. Of course, very few guesses, if any, will be as accurate as the tape measure.

CONNECTION

Just as the tape measure is the accurate, final authority on measurements, the Bible is the accurate and ultimate truth about God.

Bible Gossip

To demonstrate how the Bible was *not* transmitted—or to point out the need to read and memorize Scripture—try this.

Form a circle with 15 to 30 kids in it, each of them with a sheet of paper. Write a not-so-well-known passage of Scripture on *your* sheet of paper, then give it and your pen to the first person in the circle. He or she reads the passage, destroys the original, then writes down what they remember of the passage on their own sheet of paper. Now *this* copy and the pen are then passed to the next person who does the same, and so forth all around the circle.

The object is to see what shape the passage is in when it gets to the last person.

CONNECTION

Tell your students:

A lot of people think this is how we ended up with the Bible—through some kind of primitive gossip chain, which distorted much of the original meaning. Today we'll take a look at the Bible and its reliability.

Gettin' into the Word

S how your students several books and magazines, each designed to appeal to a certain age level and reading ability. You should have a picture book (that one would read to a baby), a comic book, a juvenile novel, a scientific journal, a college textbook, a computer instruction manual, a *TV Guide*, a GED instruction book (very fat and technical), a newspaper editorial page, and the like. (If you don't have these, you can check them out at a library.) You also need to display a big, fat Bible.

Hold up each publication in turn. Students are to rate (on a scale of 1 to 10) how hard it is to master the information in each item. Average the ratings for each book on the chalkboard.

CONNECTION

The Bible will probably be voted among the more difficult publications to master. Explain that you'll share some practical study methods and resources that will help make the Bible an open, understandable book to the average student.

Mixed Blessings

Everyone writes down what they'd like for Christmas or a birthday. Allow five or ten minutes, then ask some of the teens to read one or two of the most important items on the list.

Next, everyone lists *God's blessings or gifts to them*. Again, after five or ten minutes ask kids to describe one or two of the most important items from the list.

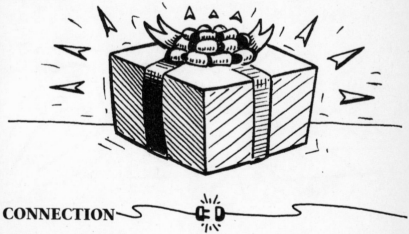

CONNECTION

Questions for discussion:
- *Was it easier to compile the birthday list or the blessing list?*
- *What benefits would you derive from the items on the birthday list? From those on the blessing list? Compare the two sets of benefits.*
- *Do you think we spend too much time wishing for material benefits?*
- *Do we spend enough time seeking God for appropriate blessings?*
- *How can we use God's blessings—tangible and otherwise—wisely?*

Appendices, Unite!

Kickstart your group into a discussion about the body of believers—the church.

When your kids arrive, give each one a slip of paper with a part of the body on it: ear, nose, foot, eye, etc. If you think of a dozen body parts but have three dozen kids, make three sets of the same body parts.

When the signal is given, kids run to form complete bodies as quickly as possible. The first group to form a complete body wins.

CONNECTION

Once the bodies are formed, proceed with small-group discussions or other activities *that require each "body" to work together as a team*—activities that, in other words, picture for your kids how the body of Christ works. An experience like this can help kids understand passages of Scripture like 1 Corinthians 12 much better.

Name That Flavor

Give your kids a box of assorted chocolates, at least one candy per person. As the kids take bites, have them tell what's inside the chocolate—nuts, cream filling, cherries, coconut, solid chocolate, etc.

CONNECTION

Your kids will make the connection when you tell them,

The blessings of God are like that—just as you discovered new treats as you bit into the chocolates, God always surprises us with his many and varied gifts as we experience him more and more.

Photocopy Mascot

Take your group to the church office. Photocopy various parts of your kids—a face, ears, elbows, hands, feet. Tape all the photocopies together to form a weird-looking paper "person," who you can use as a visual aid for just about any message dealing with human beings.

CONNECTION

Use this idea to launch a study about the importance of each person in the body of believers. As St. Paul told us, each of us serves an important purpose, just as the different parts of a human body do.

Puzzling Truth

First, put together the pieces of an inexpensive children's 50-piece or so jigsaw puzzle. Then coat it with a light-colored spray paint. Finally, with a broad, bold marker or suitable paint brush, write a message to your group—a Bible verse, an announcement for an upcoming event, anything—on the puzzle.

Now take the pieces apart and mail one or two pieces to your students, with the note, "If all the pieces to this puzzle are back in place at the end of the next meeting, I'll take all of you out for pizza—on me." Also include how they can get their puzzle pieces to the meeting if they cannot attend.

At the next meeting, start the kids fitting the puzzle together as they come in the door. If it all comes together, be prepared to shell out for a pizza party. If not, someone didn't do his or her part.

CONNECTION

The church is a body that needs all its parts to work as God designed them—if it is to function at its optimum level. We depend on each other in the community of faith.

Tell your students:

This puzzle represents the body of Christ, the church. God has designed us to be a unit—which means when parts are missing or not doing their jobs, we don't reach our potential for God. Let's take a look at how God wants to fit us all together.

21

Shoes of Christ

After your students have all sat down in a circle, ask them to take off their shoes and toss them in a pile in the middle. At your signal all students grab a pair of shoes that are *not* their own and put them on. The pairs don't have to be matching, either. Last one to get a pair of shoes on and tied is out. (Sandals are a distinct advantage in this game.) You can play this game a few times.

CONNECTION

Slipping on someone else's shoes can be difficult—or even impossible. At best it's uncomfortable—just like our positions and roles in the body of Christ, the church.

Tell your students:

We each have a shoe that fits us best. In the same way, each of us has a role within the church that fits us best. If we try to fit into a role that God didn't design for us, we'll be uncomfortable. Let's take a look at the different gifts and places we might fit in the body of Christ.

Checkered Decisions

Want to show kids how a church either enjoys or endures the consequences of decisions made by individuals in a church—or in any group or organization, for that matter?

First, dream up a bunch of silly "consequences" a team of kids can inflict on another team: howl like dogs, stand on their heads, pretend they're chickens, etc. Add to the list a few things that a team could do to *benefit* another team: back rubs, carry them around the room, and so forth.

Write these ideas on round, self-adhesive labels that you affix to the underside of a set of checkers. Set up the checkers on the checkerboard, making sure the labels are not visible.

When the meeting begins, select two teams. For each move in this checker game, a different team member gets to decide what piece to move, and where. When a team's piece is captured, that team must do what is written on the bottom of the captured checker.

CONNECTION

The Bible explains that Christians are a body whose members are interlinked with each other. Ask your students,

- *How did it make you feel when someone made a bad move in the game?*
- *Do you think it's fair that the whole group had to pay for one person's strategic mistakes?*
- *When the Bible tells us that we are a body, how do you think the poor or wise decisions of one member affects the rest of us?*

23

When I Was a Child

Here's a nostalgic Kickstarter for lessons about spiritual growth and maturity.

Ahead of time, call your students' parents and ask them to remember what their teenager's favorite childhood toy was. Armed with this information, make a two-column matching quiz: the toys down the left side, your students' names (out of order) down the right. Something like this:

___Teddy bear   A. Alice
___Slingshot   B. Thelma
___Trains   C. Reginald
___Betsy Wetsy doll   D. Henry
___Revenge of the Mario Brothers   E. Keith

Make enough copies for everyone. As kids show up for the meeting, hand the quizzes out with the instructions to match names and toys. Do this as a no-talking, no-help quiz or as a mixer where they can run around and question each other.

CONNECTION

After your match game ask your group to come up with the item that might be considered their favorite "toy" right now—whether stereos, sports equipment, motorcycles, or computers rather than teddy bears or Matchbox cars. Say something like,

The things we valued as children lose their significance as we mature. God's design is to mature us—which means some of the ideas we have about God and ourselves and each other will eventually fall away as we grow up spiritually. Let's see what God's Word has to say about growing as a Christian.

Taboos

Explain to your students some customs and taboos in other cultures:

- Don't make the okay sign (raised hand, thumb and forefinger forming a circle, other fingers pointing up) after a good meal in Brazil. You will have made an obscene gesture to your host.
- Arabs (and many Asians) will flinch if you expose the sole of your shoe. A polite person keeps his feet flat on the ground at all times, even while sitting.
- In many places in Mexico, the old "shave and a haircut, two bits" knock means you're looking for trouble.
- *Never* wear your shoes inside the house in Japan, Fiji, or Hawaii.
- In Bulgaria to nod your head yes really means no.
- In Taiwan blinking your eyes at someone is impolite.
- Women are forbidden to drive cars or bicycles in Saudi Arabia.
- Waving bye-bye in Greece will probably get you in trouble since it doesn't mean bye-bye to them.

Now see if your kids can think of any taboos in their own culture.

CONNECTION

Christians do some things differently. In many ways we are aliens in our own culture. Tell your students,

We may laugh at what seem to us weird ideas and behavior of other cultures, yet these things let us see how odd a Christian lifestyle is to those who are unfamiliar with it. Christians do their best to practice a behavior that is not of this world. Non-Christians may not understand what we're doing or why we do it.

'Tis the Season

To focus your kids on the real meaning of the Christmas story, take your kids to the mall and have them politely question shoppers with the following brief survey. When you've collected several surveys, drive back to your meeting room and discuss the results.

The Quick Christmas Survey

Ask shoppers: **Do you have time to answer 4 quick questions in our youth group's Christmas survey?**
Check one: ❏ female ❏ male
Check one: ❏ child ❏ teenager ❏ young adult ❏ adult ❏ senior

1. In your opinion, most people give Christmas gifts because—
  a. They are expected to.
  b. They show their love to friends and family by this practice.
  c. It is a reflection of God's gift of Jesus to mankind.
  d. They will get gifts in return.

2. Do you believe that Christmas is—
  a. Too commercial?
  b. Too religious?
  c. An appropriate mix of the commercial and the religious?

3. In your opinion, Santa and Christmas trees and decorations—
  a. Obscure the meaning of Christmas.
  b. Are a nice part of the season.
  c. Are symbols for deeper meanings.

4. During this season most people you know—
  a. Become stressed and frazzled.
  b. Have a chance to consider God's love for them and their love for others.
  c. Are relaxed and family-oriented.

Picture This

Use photos to kickstart a discussion on anything. Do you have a Bible study on the love of money, wealth, status? Or one on how to use resources wisely and compassionately? Flip through magazines for a picture of a fancy and expensive car, then cut it out.

At the meeting, invite your students to give one-sentence statements about what they see. You'll get all kinds of responses, from "I'd love to have one" to "I wouldn't be caught dead in one."

CONNECTION

Most kids respond to photos of things—whether cars, jeans, or computers—in ways that reveal their values. So use their responses as a bridge to a study on how to use your resources with compassion. Ask questions like these:

- *If Jesus came to earth today to minister, do you think Jesus would drive a car like this one? Why or why not?*
- *Do you think there comes a point where it's wrong to pay so much for a car?*
- *Is a Christian justified in buying leather seats, sun roofs, or other options if that money could be used to help another Christian who has <u>no</u> transportation?*

Bags of Sin

To launch a talk about confession and forgiveness, all you need is a table lamp with the shade removed, several paper lunch bags, and a felt marker.

Switch on the lamp as you explain the nature of light and illumination—especially regarding spiritual light. Now write a common sin—maybe gossip—on one of the lunch sacks. Place it over the light bulb. Label more sacks with sins (let the kids suggest the sins), layering them onto the bulb. Soon there will be only a feeble glow. Pulling the sacks off one by one represents confession and forgiveness, until the bulb's light shines brightly again.

CONNECTION

Tell your students:

When we commit a sin, it affects us spiritually—and emotionally, sometimes physically, and in other ways, too. In fact, the effects of sin can really darken our souls. Yet God can strip those sins away and heal our wounds. Confession is how we hand over our sins to God for him to deal with. He takes the sins away and we can begin to shine again.

Backbone of Jell-O

It can be tough to live a Christian life, especially in the face of criticism. Start your lesson about spiritual courage with a few of these classic Jell-O games:

- **Jell-O Eating Contest.** No hands, of course.
- **Jell-O Relay.** Players race with a cube of Jell-O balanced on their tongues.
- **Blindfold Jell-O Mine Field.** Mine the floor with Jell-O (put the Jell-O on paper plates unless you can hose down the floor). Blindfolded players must walk—or run—through minefield.
- **Blindfold Jell-O Feed.** Contestants feed each other Jell-O while blindfolded.
- **Jell-O Nail.** Before this event, put Jell-O cubes in the freezer. Teams try to nail as many Jell-O cubes to a log or board as they can.

CONNECTION

Jell-O, of course, has come to symbolize anything *but* backbone and courage—it sloppily conforms to whatever mold it finds itself in. As you head into your message, point out the similarities between cowardice and Jell-O—and then contrast those with strength of character and courage of convictions.

Door Number One, Two, or Three?

You can leap into a discussion on decision making by putting together a game show for your students.

Have one or more student volunteers come forward to receive a small prize—a candy bar or dollar, say. Ask if they'd like to trade their candy bar or dollar for what's behind a door (actually, a square of poster board taped to the wall) or in a box at your feet. Give each contestant two or three chances to trade for unknown prizes. Most of the prizes should be junk. You can play several rounds, but the volunteers must live with the final results of their decisions (just like life).

CONNECTION

Point out that we all must live with the results of our decisions—just as the contestants had to accept whatever prize they ended up with. Ask questions like these:

- *Why did you choose to trade—was it based on knowledge or a lucky feeling?*
- *Is it possible in life to be somewhat sure of the results of big decisions?*
- *What are some ways God can help us make wise decisions?*

World's Heaviest Baby

There is ample evidence for the existence of God. To get into that lesson, hand out enough copies of the *National Enquirer* or *The Star* (or another of their ilk) for each small group to have one.

Instruct the small groups to skim the articles and then rate a half dozen or so of the articles for their veracity: which articles sound true, which sound unlikely, and which are flat-out ludicrous.

CONNECTION

During this Kickstarter, lead your students into the understanding that what makes any of these stories convincing is *evidence*. The more evidence, the more likely a story will be believed. Then jump into your evidence for God's existence.

I Can't Because—

Excusing one's own misbehavior is a national pastime. Christians are just as likely to rationalize their own unwillingness to live a Christian life. This Kickstarter introduces a lesson on lame excuses and what to do about them.

Give each student two 3 x 5 index cards. On one card each student writes, "I'd like to—," filling in the blank with something they'd like to do. On the other card they write, "But I can't, because—," again completing the sentence. Inform students that these can be serious or silly (but not obscene or disrespectful).

Collect the cards, keeping the two kinds in two separate piles. Shuffle the two piles separately, then draw the top card from each pile and read the "I'd like to—" and "But I can't because—" sentences together. Everyone will get a laugh at the random combinations.

CONNECTION

Have a good laugh over these creative excuses, then move on to your lesson about excuses biblical characters used to bail out on God, excuses teenagers use to avoid Christian responsibilities, etc.

All Scrambled

Before the meeting, write your key passage on index cards, one word per card. Duplicate these (with photocopier or by simply making several sets) so there are enough card sets of the verse for every small group of four to six students.

At the meeting form the small groups, then distribute the card sets. When you give them the go-ahead, they unscramble the passage to discover the text for the day.

CONNECTION

Suppose that you are going to teach on faith. If your passage was Ephesians 2:8-9, you would scramble that verse and let your groups compete to see who could unscramble it fastest.

Carbonated Faith

Want to kickstart a lesson with a graphic demonstration of faith? Give chilled cans of soda to your kids, but do it this way: they should come to you one at a time to get their sodas. You pop the top of each can as you hand it to a student (as if your intention was to be helpful). When the last student arrives for his, make a huge show of shaking the can—then *all but* open the can under the student's nose.

Not only this student, but the first two or three rows will expect to be showered with soda. Watch 'em scatter!

CONNECTION

By running or dodging the soda, the students demonstrated an active belief. Faith in God is like that—true faith results in a dynamic, life-changing response.

Put Up or Shut Up

Give your students a "test of faith." Well, actually it's a play on words—but it will get your kids involved as your lesson on faith begins.

Show your students a closed box or bag and say, "If you touch the powder in this bag, you will die—just like that. Anybody not believe me?"

Play this to the hilt by emphasizing that you're not lying. Encourage anyone who still doesn't believe you to prove it by reaching into the bag and touching the powder. When one finally does this, congratulate her for her courage to follow through on her convictions.

And just what does the bag contain? A box of dye—which, if you touch, you can dye (by following the directions on the box).

Other objects you can claim to have in the bag:

- South American Poison Dart Frog (a map of South America, ant or rodent poison, a dart, a rubber frog)
- Rattle Snake (a baby rattle and a rubber snake)
- Bear Trap (a stuffed bear and a Roach Motel or mouse trap)
- Contact Explosive (Contac nasal spray and a firecracker)

CONNECTION

Perhaps several students said they didn't believe you—but they didn't have the courage to reach into the box or bag. Belief in Christ requires genuine trust evidenced by commitment.

Yes, Virginia

Have your group vote (keep track of votes on the chalkboard) on how many of them once believed in modern American mythical beings: the Tooth Fairy, Santa Claus, the Easter Bunny, the Stork, the Sandman, the Boogie Man, and so on. (For a lively touch to the meeting, adult volunteers can outfit themselves in appropriate costumes for each of these creatures!)

CONNECTION

Belief in Jesus is very different from belief in fictions. He is truth, and the biblical evidence for him is very compelling. Nor does he ask us to exercise blind faith—Jesus stands the tests of inquiry.

Paper Tear

If you have a large group, get together in smaller circles of eight to ten kids. Distribute scrap paper and ask students to tear it in a shape that symbolizes or represents their fathers (but no physical profiles, silhouettes, or other literalisms—symbols only).

Ask some of the kids to explain (to their small group or the whole group) what they've symbolized. *Be sensitive and cautious about who you call on to share publicly.* This is a delicate and even painful subject for some teenagers, and not one they want to talk openly about.

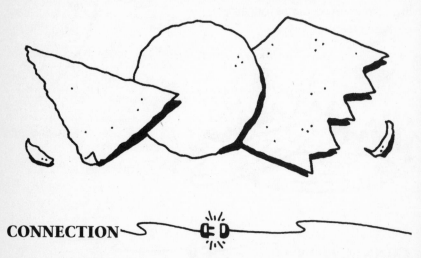

CONNECTION

Tell your students:

From a look at your shapes, I can tell that some of you will have an easier time than others with the idea of God as our Father.

Odd Man Out

Before the meeting cut a jigsaw puzzle out of plain white paper or cardboard—eight or ten pieces is enough. Cut an extra piece, too—one that looks like it belongs in the puzzle, but actually doesn't.

At the meeting recruit as many kids as there are pieces, and instruct them to assemble the puzzle in front of the group.

CONNECTION

Sooner or later, the student with the odd piece will realize that he is "odd man out" on the puzzle. Move into a discussion of cliques, favoritism, or exclusion.

Feet of Clay

You'll need a pile of Play-Doh (or modeling clay) and a flat surface to work on. Ask students to use the clay to create anything that in any way illustrates or symbolizes a fear people their age have. Give them a few minutes to think about this idea before they begin. Invite them to explain to the group what they've created.

CONNECTION

Only a fool doesn't fear. Unfortunately, though, some live in a climate of self-imposed fear—a fear that God can solve. Tell your students,

You've created some tangible symbols of an average kid's fears. Today we'll look at this very human tendency to get bogged down or even paralyzed by fear.

Food for Thought

Food always succeeds as a meeting kickstarter. For example, try these delicious recipes:

- **humble pie eating contest.** Have volunteers dig into pies in front of a banner proclaiming HUMBLE PIE EATING CONTEST. A fun lead-in to a talk on humility.
- **Bread of Life.** Many pizza restaurants sell tasty, soft bread sticks made out of pizza dough, with pizza sauce to dip them into. Serve these as you begin a talk on Christ, the bread of life.
- **Living Water.** Serve clear sodas, or water that you blend with powdered drink mix.
- **Fruit of the Holy Spirit.** Bring some exotic fruit to the meeting to serve as you teach: mangos, kiwi fruit, and such. Or make fresh fruit smoothies (blend one scoop crushed ice, one frozen or fresh banana, your choice of fruit, and a little juice).

Crossword Pals

Kickstart a lesson on friendship by creating your own crossword puzzle, with the names of your students as the answers in the puzzle. For clues, use unusual facts about the kids that aren't widely known. (You can get such facts at an earlier meeting by having the kids write down something unusual about themselves.)

Later, as you read the answers, ask students if they want to add any more details about their clues.

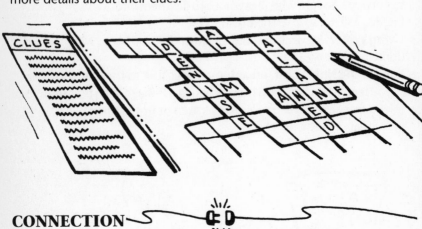

CONNECTION

Say something like,

It's great to get to know people. The better we know each other, the stronger the bonds of friendship. Let's dig into the Bible to examine some friends we find there—and some principles of friendship.

Balloon Time

Balloons mean parties, parties are celebrations, and celebrations are fun. Kickstart your message on fun (or godly fun, or the dangers of the world's version of fun, etc.) by playing one or more balloon games. Some examples:

- **Balloon Stomp.** Tie balloons to ankles—the object is to stomp everyone's balloon but keep your own safe.
- **Balloon Basketball.** Kids sit in chairs as shown below and try to bat the balloon over the opposite team's heads and into the end zone.

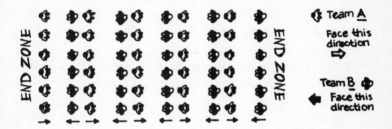

- **Balloon Stuff.** Cram underinflated balloons into your team's clothes. Most balloons wins.

CONNECTION

After you've calmed everyone down, seat them in a circle and say something like,

We've had fun playing balloon games. Everybody likes to have fun. Does the Bible talk about fun? Does God even want us to have fun? Let's get into this important issue—after all, it may be fun!

Once you're into your lesson and want students to respond to your questions, use—what else?—a balloon. Inflate a balloon and pinch it closed while you ask your question. Get the students passing a "hot potato" around the circle. You release the balloon, letting it jet around the room—and whoever holds the "potato" when the balloon hits the ground must answer your question.

Career Clues

O n 3 x 5 cards kids list three or four clues about the careers they think they will pursue in the next few years. The clues can be funny or serious, but the career possibilities should be sincere.

Collect the cards, then give each kid a sheet of paper and a pencil, and have them number down the margin as high as there are students in the group. Read the clues from the first card and have everyone write down a guess about who that person is. Remind everyone not to reveal their guesses. Repeat any cards as needed for clarity.

Now read through the cards again, only this time the students identify their cards. The results just may surprise a few people.

CONNECTION

You may want to transition to your lesson about the future with questions like these:

- *What do teenagers fear about the future?*
- *What worries you most about the future?*
- *Read Matthew 6:25-34. Do you think God wants you to worry about the future? Why or why not?*
- *What hope does God offer for your future?*

Codes

Simple codes for students to solve are a fun way to start any study. Scramble the words in a Bible passage...display a list of symbols that represent letters...cut a message into a jigsaw puzzle...you name it.

Say you wanted to teach about putting your life together after a shattering experience: have kids put together a jigsaw puzzle on which you've written a message (see **Puzzling Truth**, page 21).

Ten Years and Counting

Kids like to think about their futures—many wonder if they even have one. This Kickstarter can begin a talk that assures kids that God cares about our futures—and that he has given a future to each of us. Give each student a copy of page 47 and let them answer away.

CONNECTION

If the kids don't mind sharing, go around the group and discuss the quiz. Otherwise have the students turn them in unsigned, shuffle them, and discuss them anonymously.

10 Years from Now...

Write down what you think your life will be like in 10 years.

- My height:

- My weight:

- My hairstyle:

- Where I'll be living:

- What I'll be doing:

- The goals I'll be working toward:

- In 10 years I'll feel I have been a success in life if—

- In 10 years I'll look back upon this year as a year of—

My Coat of Arms

In ancient days people symbolized their family values and philosophies on coats of arms or crests. This Kickstarter launches a lesson about the God who knows us and uses our abilities for his purposes.

Grab some card stock paper and a sample or two of what a coat of arms can look like. Provide colored pencils and markers. Tell your students,

Create a coat of arms that depicts a few things that are significant about yourself. Be prepared to share it with the rest of the group.

CONNECTION

When they've finished creating their crests, have your students explain the significant symbols in them to the rest of the group. Move into your lesson by saying something like,

We've seen a number of unique symbols that represent talents, interests, and experiences. It was God, you know, who created us, knows us, and has given us these abilities, interests, and gifts. He wants to use us personally and uniquely.

Ingredients of Our Faith

U se this Kickstarter when you would like to discuss the attributes of a godly life.

Collect a variety of canned or packaged foodstuffs. All of it should have ingredient labels. The ingredients are listed by proportion—that is, the first ingredient listed is the main constituent of the product.

The labels can be surprising. At the start of class, pass around the food and ask your group to look at what is in each of the foods. See if you can come up with a list of the top five foods based on healthy ingredients and the bottom five based on poorest ingredients.

CONNECTION

What is important to your students? What occupies their time and attention? Where does God fit into their picture?

Ask them:

If you were to wake up one morning with the ingredients of your lives mysteriously imprinted on your skin, what might it say? Each Christian life carries some kind of nourishment for a sick world. Let's examine some of those ingredients as they're found in God's Word.

Hide and Seek

P lay this classic to open a Bible study about how God seeks us—even when we hide.

An old-fashioned game of hide and seek needs nothing but some places to hide (like the church grounds or building), the right time (night is best), and willing players. Make sure to have a home base kids can touch to become "free." Play a round or two, and then get everyone together for the Bible study.

CONNECTION

It is the nature of God to seek us even when we don't want to be found. Ask your kids starter questions like these:

- *Can you usually pick a good hiding place where you won't be found, or do you get caught all the time?*
- *Would this game be more fun if the hunters were armed with paint-ball guns and could shoot you rather than tag you? Why or why not?*
- *Do you ever see God as the seeker and you as the hider? Have you ever felt like you were hiding from God?*

Say to your students,

Today we'll take a look at a God who loves us so much, he won't let us hide from him.

Acrostic Scrambler

A simple acrostic lets your kids have fun discovering the subject of your lesson.

Write out a simple acrostic like the one below and photocopy enough copies for your students—or display it on an overhead projector, whiteboard, etc. Kids must guess the correct word, then unscramble the *first letters* of each word to discover your lesson's topic.

This example is easy, but you can make acrostics as difficult as you like, depending on your time or subject matter.

_ _ _ _ _   The central place in some churches. *(altar)*
_ _ _ _   What you receive at Christmas. *(gift)*
_ _ _ _ _   Herman Munster's child. *(Eddie)*
_ _ _ _ _ _   The species that the cartoon Bugs belongs to. *(rabbit)*
_ _ _ _ _ _   What smoking can give you. *(cancer)*

The first letters of each word—AGERC—can be unscrambled to spell GRACE.

Undeserved Favor

Randomly choose a student to come forward. Give her a simple but appreciated gift—like a favorite snack. Let her return to her seat only long enough for you to say, "Oh, I forgot—come here again." When the student returns, give her a soda. Do this whole routine several times, adding gifts  such as money, a church or youth group T-shirt, an inexpensive New Testament, and the like.

CONNECTION

Jump into your lesson by pointing out that God is gracious to all of us, whether or not we think we deserve his favor.

The Impossible Promise

Influences both positive and negative sway the thinking of your students. This Kickstarter launches a study on influences, with the goal being stable students who are less likely to be swayed from God's path.

Have your kids look through magazines and find ads that make subtle or overt claims that their products will in some way make a person's life more cool, more successful—in any case, better than their lives are now.

CONNECTION

Discuss these ads and how they attempt to influence us. Point out that all around them are people and pressures that work hard to sway peoples' attitudes, opinions, and behavior. Christians need to be alert.

Photo Ops

C ut out of magazines a dozen or so photos of several types of people—old, young, attractive, ugly...of different races, of different economic standings, and so on. Number the photos. Ask kids to write down a word or short phrase to describe their impression of the people in each of the photos. Students can work individually or in groups. Collect the papers, then list on a chalkboard the consensus of the group's opinions.

CONNECTION

Discuss questions and issues like these:
- *Which five people would you most want to have as friends? Why?*
- *Is there any one person you'd want <u>nothing</u> to do with?*
- *Which five people look most likely to be Christians?*
- *Which person seems most like you?*
- *What do you think these people do for a living or for fun?*

   Now move into your subject—the problem of judging others primarily by looks.

Pie in the Face

In 2 Timothy 1:11-12 St. Paul says he knows Jesus Christ. Notice the apostle doesn't say he knows stuff *about* Jesus Christ. Some of your students may know quite a bit *about* the Lord without actually knowing Jesus himself.

As you begin explaining this to your group, arrange for an adult who's a stranger to your students (or someone who can be effectively *disguised* as a stranger to your students) run shouting into the room, spray you with soda or shove a cream pie in your face, then run out of the room.

Now (that is, once you've got the pie at least out of your eyes) ask the kids to answer specific questions about the attacker. How many can tell the color of the attacker's shoes? Was he or she wearing a belt? What did the person say, word for word? How long did the incident last?

CONNECTION

Just as no one student can recall completely the details of this event, many Christians don't have a clear and detailed knowledge of Jesus Christ. But that's all right (for now, at least), for knowing facts about Christ may not be as important in the long run as actually knowing Christ.

It's the Law!

Is your lesson about God's rules, precepts, or principles? Try this Kickstarter.

Read the following laws (or write them on the chalkboard, overhead, etc.). When your kids come into the room, hand them a sheet of paper and ask them to guess which of these laws are true and which are false. The correct answers? *All* these laws are actually on the books, but rarely if ever enforced.

- You cannot play hopscotch on Missouri sidewalks on Sundays.
- You cannot hunt moths under streetlights in Los Angeles.
- In Muskegon, Michigan, it is against the law for a baseball team to hit a ball over the fence or out of the park.
- You cannot catch mice without a hunting license in Cleveland.
- In Pueblo, Colorado, you cannot grow dandelions within the city limits.
- In Gary, Indiana, you cannot go to the theater within four hours of eating garlic.
- If you eat peanuts in church in Massachusetts, you break the law.
- Daytime swimming in a pool or river is forbidden in Durango, Colorado.

CONNECTION

People make laws that often don't make sense—or if they did once, they don't now. The Bible, on the other hand, explains that God's laws and rules are "perfect, reviving the soul" (Psalm 19:7). His rules and precepts make good sense and help us live better with each other and with our Creator.

A Light to My Feet

This Kickstarter works best at night. Before your students arrive, turn off all the lights in the room and in the hallway leading to the room. Cover the windows so that the room is pitch black. Assign a staff person at each light switch to make sure kids don't tamper with them. Have one person guide students through the hall and into the room, where you'll conduct the meeting—in the dark.

CONNECTION

Use a penlight to get things started. In fact, think about using it for the entire lesson. Say to your students,

If you haven't guessed by now, this evening we are going to be talking about Jesus being a light that shines in spiritual darkness.

57

Turn Out the Lights

G ames played with blindfolds or in the dark make good Kickstarters for lessons on God's light versus spiritual darkness.

Tasks that are simple with your eyes open can be nearly impossible in the dark. For example, have blindfolded kids try to locate candy bars on the floor. A simple maze on the chalkboard is easy to trace in the light, but hopeless if you're blindfolded—without the verbal assistance of "seeing kids," that is.

CONNECTION

After your group has tried simple tasks with their eyes covered, and then again with eyes open, explain how walking in God's light makes a huge difference.

Cartoons in the Dark

Ask everyone to close their eyes—and then draw a cartoonish car, house, or other familiar object. When they're finished, let them look at their results (which are probably not too good). Now have students work in pairs: the drawer with pencil in hand and eyes closed, and the "navigator" to explain to the "blind" drawer how to make the image.

CONNECTION

Say to your students,

> *Just as you did a much better job of drawing when you had someone to guide you, God can guide us through life much better than we can grope through it alone.*

The Fly

This Kickstarter sets *you* up as a living object lesson.

Walk into the youth room and begin the meeting with your fly open...or with a corner of your shirttail caught in your fly...or with a smudge of lipstick on your teeth...or with a glob of mascara plastered just below your eye. Your first words are a prepared introduction on the subject of friendship, and how true friends help friends out of embarrassing situations.

Walk around the class, smile brightly and frequently—do anything to make your fashion gaffe noticeable. See how long it takes before someone actually says something. If they merely signal you in one way or another, ignore them or play dumb to their signals. When someone comments (or when no one comments), drop the act and explain that you intentionally baited them to see if anyone had the courage and concern to talk to you.

CONNECTION

Tell your group,

Today we'll look at the difficult job of speaking the truth in a loving way. This is not always easy, but as you can see by my little experiment today, it is sometimes necessary.

Observation Game

A quick Kickstarter that directs discussion toward the topic of Christian love.

Send one student out of the room. While he's gone, ask others to tell things about his appearance: what kind of shoes, pants, and other clothing was he wearing? What color are his eyes? Does he wear glasses? An earring? Write down the group's recollections on a chalkboard—then call the person back into the room and see how many are correct.

If you want, prime someone ahead of time so she can wear distinctive clothes, accessories, etc.

CONNECTION

Use this game to introduce the idea of thinking and caring about each other. Tell your students,

A lot of people wander through life and never pay much mind to people around them. They don't notice those who are lonely, hurting—or those with really great potential. God wants to help us be more alert to those around us and to care for them as we would ourselves.

Wallet Exchange

Ready to teach about love for others—to the point of enlarging one's circle of friends?

Ask your students to get out their wallets, exchange them with someone else, and then thumb their neighbors' wallets. Just two rules: 1) Take note of what you find in the wallet. 2) Don't steal anything.

Your kids will discover that, besides money and I.D., wallets contain personal mementos: photos, keepsakes, and the like. Ask your students, *What besides money did you notice in your friend's wallet? If you saw pictures, who were they of?*

Be prepared for some unusual items to be named—pictures of pets or strange doodads in their wallets.

CONNECTION

Explain to your students,

In wallets you'll often find what's valuable to the owners. Money and I.D. cards are there, and probably the photos of valuable friends. Now we'll consider how we can show God's love to those people and friends whose pictures have yet to make their way into our wallets.

Bad Company

To get your group thinking about loving the unlovely, create a huge poster to hang in the room: ABSOLUTELY *NOT* ON MY PARTY LIST. Have markers available. When kids come into the room, ask them to write on the

poster a few names of famous people—contemporary or historical—that they would *never* want at a party with them. Only one condition: they cannot repeat a name that already appears on the poster. In no time you should have a pretty good list of nefarious characters.

CONNECTION

Jesus himself partied with the very kinds of people that most of us would rather stay away from. Jump into a Bible study about Christ's mandate to love those who are unlovely. Be sure to deal with practical things kids can do to show God's love.

Wanted!

What sort of behavior should mark individuals as Christians? Stop by your local post office to see if they'll give you (or allow you to make copies of) some of the FBI fliers of felons posted in their lobby. You may get some out-of-date ones, or they may even let you take some right off the wall if you explain why you want them.

Before your meeting hang up the wanted posters around the room. Chances are, curiosity will drive your kids to read them all.

CONNECTION

Wanted men and women are described in detail on the posters. Similarly, our lives need to be distinctive enough to provide evidence of our faith.

Tell your students,

Someone once wondered that, if it were a crime to be a Christian, would there be enough evidence to convict those who call themselves by that name. You can see from the posters that most of these alleged bad guys have distinguishing features—scars maybe, or habits. Let's consider what marks show us to be believers in an unbelieving world.

The People Who Brought You This Book...

invite you to discover MORE valuable youth-ministry resources

Youth Specialties offers an assortment of books, publications, tapes, and events, all designed to encourage and train youth workers and their kids. Just return this card, and we'll send you FREE information on our products and services.

Please send me the FREE Youth Specialties Catalog and information on upcoming Youth Specialties events.

Are you: ❏ A volunteer youth worker (or) ❏ A salaried youth worker   480001

Name _____ Title _____

Church/Organization _____

Address: ❏ Home (or) ❏ Church _____

City _____ State ____ Zip _____

Phone Number: ❏ Home (or) ❏ Church (_____)_____

E-Mail address _____

The People Who Brought You This Book...

invite you to discover MORE valuable youth-ministry resources

Youth Specialties offers an assortment of books, publications, tapes, and events, all designed to encourage and train youth workers and their kids. Just return this card, and we'll send you FREE information on our products and services.

Please send me the FREE Youth Specialties Catalog and information on upcoming Youth Specialties events.

Are you: ❏ A volunteer youth worker (or) ❏ A salaried youth worker   480001

Name _____ Title _____

Church/Organization _____

Address: ❏ Home (or) ❏ Church _____

City _____ State ____ Zip _____

Phone Number: ❏ Home (or) ❏ Church (_____)_____

E-Mail address _____

Call toll-free to order:
(800) 776-8008

BUSINESS REPLY MAIL
FIRST-CLASS MAIL   PERMIT 268   HOLMES PA

POSTAGE WILL BE PAID BY ADDRESSEE

NO POSTAGE
NECESSARY
IF MAILED
IN THE
UNITED STATES

YOUTH SPECIALTIES
P.O. BOX 668
HOLMES, PA 19043-0668

Call toll-free to order:
(800) 776-8008

BUSINESS REPLY MAIL
FIRST-CLASS MAIL   PERMIT 268   HOLMES PA

POSTAGE WILL BE PAID BY ADDRESSEE

NO POSTAGE
NECESSARY
IF MAILED
IN THE
UNITED STATES

YOUTH SPECIALTIES
P.O. BOX 668
HOLMES, PA 19043-0668

Silence of the Lambs

This Kickstarter is easier for you than for your kids (particularly if they're junior highers).

As your group enters the room, greet them with a "Shhhh!" and whispered instructions to be absolutely silent until they're given permission to speak. The awkwardness of sitting around in silence will be very odd for many of them, and impossible for some. Gently enforce the rule of silence. If you can, remove those who won't cooperate to another activity in another room.

After five minutes (or 10 if you're daring) break the silence and allow kids to let off some steam.

CONNECTION

In our culture we are surrounded by noise from the time we get up to the time we go to bed. Silence can be so unusual that it makes many kids (and adults) feel uncomfortable.

Ask your students some questions before beginning a Bible study on using silence to meditate before the Lord.
- *Was it uncomfortable for you to be silent? Why or why not?*
- *How often are you intentionally silent?*
- *What are some good things that we can learn from being silent before God?*

Spot the Dog

This idea kickstarts any lesson that qualifies as a mystery—the Trinity, the Incarnation, etc.

Before class buy a bag of individually wrapped candies. Then photocopy page 67. Hang the picture on the wall with the caption, FIGURE OUT WHAT THIS IS A PICTURE OF, TELL ME PRIVATELY WHAT IT IS, AND WIN A PRIZE.

As kids come into the class, direct them to the picture. Stay on the other side of the room and let students come to you and quietly tell you what's in the picture.

If they've got it right, toss 'em a chunk of candy and tell them to keep quiet.

Can you see the dog? Look again:

CONNECTION

The spiritual world is full of things that we can't see, at least in the literal sense. As we adjust to walking by the power of the Holy Spirit though, we begin to catch on to what God is doing and see his hand in ways we never could before.

Tell your students,

If you saw a picture of a Dalmatian with its nose to the ground, you are correct. If you saw anything else, you have a vivid imagination. Today we will consider a truth about God that some might call a mystery—because either it takes a while before you really understand it, or else it's simply not understandable, period.

Spot the Dog

What's in a Name?

Before your meeting, swing into a bookstore or library and find one of those Name Your Baby books. The book should include meanings of names, too. (Used bookstores usually have scads of these.)

With the book as your guide, start telling kids what their first names mean. Discuss which names are common or unoriginal, which have humorous or embarrassing meanings, etc. Ask your students what they would name themselves if they could change their names right now.

CONNECTION

God has more than one name. In fact, the Bible is filled with his titles. Tell your group,

We know each other by names—and we know God by his names, too. Let's create a list of God's names as we find them in the Bible.

Do Not Touch

Here's an easy way to kickstart a lesson about the human sin nature. In the center of a sheet of paper, glue a push-button (or a fuzzy little ball, or a similar small goody). On the paper print in large letters, DO NOT TOUCH, with an arrow pointing to the button. Tape the paper to the wall of your meeting room. Arrange for one student to covertly jot down the names of those who touch the button despite the sign's warning.

When you are ready to begin class, get the list of kids who touched the button and be prepared to humorously give them a hard time for their "sin."

Want a more grandiose version of this Kickstarter? Screw the push-button to a board, and actually wire it to a battery and a car horn; just be sure to hide the wiring, the battery, and the horn. The first culprit to touch the button will start your lesson with a blast.

CONNECTION

We tend to wonder at the stupidity of Adam and Eve—they had it all, but just couldn't *not* sin. Yet we're more like them than we think. Tell your students,

You see by this list of people who touched the DO NOT TOUCH *button that we're inclined to do the very thing that we're not supposed to do. The Bible calls this our "sin nature." It means that we're preprogrammed, so to speak, to reach out and touch forbidden things. But God has made a way for us to deal with, cope with, even live <u>above</u> that sin nature.*

A Bird in the Hand

Kick off a study of any of the parables with this. Before class write on the chalkboard or overhead projector a whole pile of aphorisms, maxims, and proverbs—like the ones on page 71, which you can reproduce for each student, photocopy into a transparency, or simply select a few from.

As kids come into the class, hand them paper and pencils and ask them to write down in simple English the meaning of the proverbs. Reward the kid who does the best job.

CONNECTION

Jesus used parables and proverbs like these to get his point across—consequently, his listeners sometimes only "sorta got" what he meant. Say to your group,

Now we'll look at a teaching of Jesus that may have seemed as vague to his audience as some of these saying were to you.

Ancient Sayings You Oughta Know

What do they say in simple, modern English?

1. You can lead a horse to water, but you can't make him drink.
2. A rolling stone gathers no moss.
3. Oil and water don't mix.
4. A penny saved is a penny earned.
5. Nothing ventured, nothing gained.
6. Early to bed, early to rise, makes a man healthy, wealthy and wise.
7. The love of money is the root of all evil.
8. A stitch in time saves nine.
9. A watched pot never boils.
10. If at first you don't succeed, try, try again.
11. The squeaky wheel gets the grease.
12. Spare the rod and spoil the child.
13. Seek and ye shall find.
14. He who hesitates is lost.
15. Beauty is only skin deep.
16. Make hay while the sun shines.
17. It's too late to close the barn door after the horse escapes.
18. A city set on a hill cannot be hidden.
19. Necessity is the mother of invention.
20. A friend in need is a friend indeed.
21. A bird in the hand is worth two in the bush.
22. Silence is golden.
23. Children should be seen and not heard.
24. Don't cast your pearls before swine.
25. What's good for the goose is good for the gander.
26. A fool and his money are soon parted.
27. You can't judge a book by its cover.
28. Pretty is as pretty does.
29. Don't count your chickens before they hatch.
30. Cleanliness is next to godliness.
31. Where there's smoke there's fire.
32. Patience is a virtue.
33. Time and tide wait for no man.
34. Don't cry over spilt milk.
35. Still water runs deep.
36. Age is no respecter of persons.
37. Don't put off till tomorrow what you can do today.
38. It's an ill wind that blows no good.
39. People who live in glass houses shouldn't throw stones.
40. Let sleeping dogs lie.
41. Never look a gift horse in the mouth.
42. It isn't over till the fat lady sings.

From *Kickstarters* by Rick Bundschuh and Tom Finley. Permission to reproduce this page granted only for use in your own youth group. Youth Specialties, 1224 Greenfield Dr., El Cajon, CA 92021.

Scrambled Eggs

If your lesson is about the need to be careful with delicate, fragile things—whether those things are God's commands, the students' own minds or bodies, difficult relationships, etc.—this Kickstarter will do the job.

Select three volunteers to participate, you say, in a rope-jumping contest. But just as they're about to begin, stop them: "Oh, I forgot one detail. The jumper must hold an egg between her teeth as she jumps. And the winner is the one of the three who can survive the yokey mess, or at least do the most jumps before the egg cracks in her mouth.

Be sure to gradually accelerate the rope, pushing each jumper to jump faster and faster.

CONNECTION

Clean up the mess—then on to the need to deal carefully with whatever fragile, delicate thing your lesson is about.

Things Are Looking Up

A fast, effective way to introduce any Bible study. You'll need a dozen or so sheets of card stock, felt pens, a ladder, and some heavy-duty tape or push-pins.

Before class write a sentence, phrase, or Bible verse that introduces your study, one word per sheet of paper. Tape the words randomly around the ceiling of the room.

As kids come into the room, they will eventually spot the lesson on the ceiling. Give a small prize (a thrift store neck brace?) to the kid who figures out the message first.

Spinning a Good Yarn

To introduce just about any Bible study topic, run yarn in different directions from a central point throughout the room—twine it around chairs, ceiling fixtures, tables, then out the door, down the hall, and as far as you want. The distant end of each length of yarn is attached to a sheet of paper or envelope that contains hints to the message, Bible verses, or the like. Your students will have fun trying to follow their team's string to the goal.

CONNECTION

Reassemble the group to compare or solve what each team has discovered at the end of the strings. Point out that your message will help them untangle important facts God wants them to know.

Misfortune Cookies

Use this Kickstarter for a Bible lesson about the blessings of God on your students—and their obligation to others who have less.

First, buy enough fortune cookies for everyone in your group. Then write your own fortunes, both "wealthy" and "poor" ones. To represent the small proportion of people in the world who are wealthy, only five percent of the fortunes you write should be "wealthy" ones—like YOU ARE A BLUE BLOOD WHO JUST INHERITED A MILLION BUCKS. YOU WILL RECEIVE COOKIES FROM MANY WHO ARE LESS FORTUNATE THAN YOU. DO NOT SHARE YOUR COOKIES WITH ANYONE. Write these on blue slips.

Half the cookies should have "poor" fortunes—like YOU HAVE TO GO TO BED HUNGRY. FIND SOMEONE WHO HAS A BLUE FORTUNE AND GIVE YOUR COOKIE TO THEM. Write these fortunes on white paper strips.

For the remaining cookies, write fortunes like YOU CAN KEEP YOUR COOKIE, OR YOU CAN SHARE IT WITH SOMEONE WHO HAS NONE. Use a third color of paper for these fortunes. Tweezers can help you get the slips into the cookies.

The upshot, of course, is that the world's benefits, wealth, and opportunities are distributed very unevenly among the world's peoples.

As kids come into the room, instruct them to take a cookie and discover their fortune. Tell them to be sure to follow the instructions, to the letter.

CONNECTION

Your group is acting out with fortune cookies the lot of most of this planet's people. God has probably blessed most of your group with far more than any other people in the world. But it comes with a price: the obligation to be generous with what we've been given. Tell your students,

You can see from this cookie exchange that the fortunes of many are very poor. What obligations do those who call themselves Christians have toward those who have little or nothing?

You're Not Just Whistlin' Dixie

With God, the Bible says, nothing is impossible. Give your group a crack at something impossible.

Give participants several soda crackers, each with a thick layer of

peanut butter. Everyone stuffs three or four crackers into their mouths and immediately tries to whistle a familiar tune. Give them a 30-second time limit.

CONNECTION

Say something like—

This silly dare simply reminds us that not all things are possible for humans. But with God __all__ things are possible. Let's take a look in the Bible at one or two incredible things God has done.

The Great Button Controversy

How do your students feel that peer pressure affects them? Put a dozen or so buttons in a box and then pass the box around the group. Have each student silently count the buttons and remember how many were in the box. Instruct each person to reach into the box and feel the buttons as they count.

By prior arrangement, have the next-to-the-last person remove one button from the box secretly so that the last person's count is off by one. Probably everyone will come up with the same number of buttons except the last person. Take the box and set it away. See if the group can convince the last person to change his mind about the number of buttons.

CONNECTION

Pressure from the culture in general and peers in particular can make us let go of what we know is truly correct. Use this Kickstarter to guide your group toward a Bible study about peer pressure, integrity, or righteous living in a dark world.

The Great Celebrity Makeover

Okay, this Kickstarter's on the strange side, but it's a fun way to get into a lesson about pride, vanity, or focusing on one's outward beauty.

Get a pile of magazines with photos of people on the covers. Fashion magazines are great—*Elle, Vogue, Good Housekeeping, YM, Seventeen*, even *Working Woman*—but don't neglect news magazines (*Time* and *Newsweek* usually carry people on their covers), sports magazines (there are *always* people on the cover of *Sports Illustrated*), magazines that cover popular culture (*Rolling Stone, Entertainment Weekly, People Magazine*), etc. Provide your students with erasers, pencils, fine-point markers, and table space.

Start the meeting by inviting the kids to take part in the Great Celebrity Makeover Contest. Show them how to lightly erase any features from the people on the covers of a magazine and—with the tools provided—create a brand-new look for them. (You may want to create one or two yourself ahead of time, as models for what can be done.) Ask an adult from outside the youth group to come in and judge the best Celebrity Makeover when your students have finished. The prize? A huge Pink Pearl eraser.

CONNECTION

The American obsession with our looks is actually paper thin and can be altered quickly by the eraser of time. Tell your students,

It's fun to mess with the faces of the Beautiful People on magazine covers—especially when you think of what their beauty means to the models and celebrities. Yet sooner or later, if they want to hold on to a youthful, wrinkle-free beauty that is more or less natural now, these gorgeous women and studly men will be making appointments with a plastic surgeon. What does the Bible say about inner versus outer beauty?

Curious Curios

S how your students a dozen or so old odds and ends you've picked up from a thrift store—unusual tools, parts from an old machine of some sort, strange cooking utensils, antique curios—as long as you include some puzzlers, whose purpose is hard to figure out from just looking at it. Give everyone a chance to hazard a guess on the purpose of each thing.

CONNECTION

Say something like,

> *Just as these weird thingies each have a purpose, so God has made you and me (also a little weird), each of us with an important reason for being.*

What's It For?

Bring a few common objects to class and give a silly demonstration of their alternative uses—using a hairbrush to brush your teeth (after squeezing out a l-o-n-g string of toothpaste onto the brush)...using bright red lipstick for eyeliner...doing your best to cut your fingernails or toenails with rose clippers—or better yet, a big pair of hedge clippers.

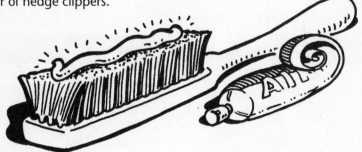

CONNECTION

God has a well-thought-out, very special purpose for all of us. But as long as we insist on doing just our own thing, we aren't fulfilling our purpose in life.

Drive Your Point Home

Ask a friend or church member to park their 'Vette, Porsche, Mercedes, or Lamborghini in the church parking lot during your youth group meeting. (In a pinch, your '81 Dodge Dart will do.) After you've asked students to list the benefits of owning a car—you can go where you like when you like, no more mooching rides or hopping the bus, you can drive your friends around—walk out to the parking lot and gather around your friend's car.

After you've oohed and ahhed over the computer-regulated engine, the electric headlight wipers, etc., move into a discussion about the responsibilities a driver must shoulder—the steering wheel and accelerator represent the responsibility to drive safely, the gas tank speaks of the cost involved, the seat belts suggest safety, the engine and tires represent the responsibility of maintenance, the paint job speaks of cleaning, and so on.

CONNECTION

You can take this Kickstarter anywhere you want—the benefits and responsibilities of dating, of being a Christian, etc. Tell your students,

Owning and operating a car requires us to be responsible. We face many areas in life in which we must be careful to do things the right way. Let's talk about one of those areas now.

Build-It-Yourself Babel

The Tower of Babel is an appropriate story for conveying a salvation message.

Bring a few bags of potatoes and several boxes of strong toothpicks (or large finishing nails) to your study—then let teams compete to build the highest, most awesome tower of potatoes, held together with the toothpicks.

CONNECTION

Congratulate the architects and engineers, then move into your study: the futility of trying to reach God by sheer human effort. The ancient builders of the Tower of Babel had no more success building a stairway to God than your group just did. Only Christ gets us to God.

Which Side Are You On?

Use this Kickstarter, a simple one that gets kids up and involved, for any number of subjects.

Divide your room into sections: an AGREE section, a DISAGREE section, and an I DUNNO section. The sections may be walls of your room.

Gather everyone in the center of the room. When you read a statement, the kids walk to whichever section or wall best represents their point of view—that is, whether they agree with your statement, disagree with it, or aren't sure. Encourage kids not to merely follow their friends but to go to the section that best describes their viewpoints on the statements you are about to make.

Say your study is about heaven and hell. You might make statements like these:

• You can believe in God and still go to hell.
• One can never know in this life who went to heaven and who went to hell.
• Everyone is guaranteed at least one chance to believe in God—and thus escape hell.
• No one is beyond God's saving grace—not even Adolf Hitler.
• The idea of a hot and fiery hell is traditional, not biblical.

By the time you ask a dozen or so questions, the kids will have moved around the room several times.

This Kickstarter, by the way, can be used the week or two *before* your lesson on the subject, in order to find out just how much your group knows about the topic you'll teach on. What you discover about their beliefs can guide your lesson preparation.

Adam's Apple

S tart your study of the Fall (Genesis 3) with this relay. Team members sink their teeth into an apple and trot it to their teammates across the room—and transfer the apple to them mouth to mouth, without hands. Even if an apple is dropped midway, the player must use only her teeth to grab it again.

CONNECTION

It probably wasn't an apple that Adam and Eve bit into. But they did bite into Satan's lie.

Worth a Thousand Words

Christ wants his people to be ready for his return, whenever and however that occurs. Make this point bigtime with the help of a vidcam and the permission of your kids' parents: be there in their rooms when the kids are awakened in the morning. Absolute surprise, of course, is essential. Be sure to pan the vidcam around some of the messier rooms, too.

CONNECTION

Video cameras don't lie. Tell your kids,

This video shows some of you at your worst time of the day. If you had known I was coming—that would have been a different story. Some of you would have been dressed, had your teeth and hair brushed, and been in the kitchen instead of your bedroom. Let's look now at Christ's warning for us to be ready for his return to Earth.

Find the Teacher

Here's a Kickstarter that will have your kids scrambling all over the church to be part of your group.

Before the meeting prepare a number of clues that ultimately lead your kids from the normal meeting room to an unusual nook where you're hiding—and where you'll hold the meeting (the boiler room, say, or the nursery, or the Fireside Room—in which case you can climb into the fireplace itself, draw the spark curtain closed, and *really* make the adolescent Sherlocks work to find you!).

The clues can be easy or difficult, symbolic or coded—it's your call—as long as the students can figure out where to go, from clue to clue, and eventually find you. Assign an adult sponsor or two to scoot along with the kids in their search for you.

CONNECTION

Kids won't find you unless they really work at it. Much the same way, people don't discover God unless they seek him. And face it: God is more fun to find than you are!

True Seekers

Be prepared to part with a $20 bill and a bit of change for this Kickstarter.

Before the meeting tape a $20 bill to the bottom of a chair and scatter a few coins of various values around the room. When kids show up, casually complain that you just discovered a hole in your pocket—and most of your change fell out somewhere.

Tell your students, hey, no big loss—whatever change they can find, they can keep. (Note how few of them will really look for it.) Then fabricate some excuse to check a coat pocket, and exclaim, "Whoa! Now the $20 bill I put in my coat pocket is gone, too. Sheesh. Oh, well, if you find it, you might as well keep that, too."

Unless yours is a Beverly Hills youth group, *this* should get them out of their seats and tearing up the room to find the lost money.

CONNECTION

When the bill has been discovered, sit everyone down and tell your students,

Did you notice that most of you looked according to how much you valued the lost money? For the dime, you looked a dime's worth. For the twenty bucks, you looked twenty bucks worth. People seek God only as much as they value him. If someone feels they don't need God—as many of you felt about the dimes and nickels—that person will probably not seek him. On the other hand, someone who really wants a relationship with him will tear up the landscape to find him.

Breaking Up Isn't *That* Hard to Do

While you describe the shattering effects of sin on individuals, families, and societies, do some literal shattering of your own—of plates, bowls, and vases. (Ceramic may be a mite safer to shatter than glass.)

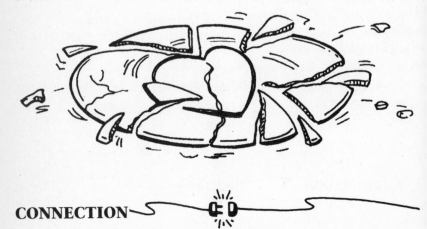

CONNECTION

To extend the metaphor, choose one plate to superglue back together—all the time pointing out the difficulty of trying to mend broken lives. God, though, can give us a whole new life—at which point you pull out a brand new, unshattered plate.

Missing the Mark

A rm your kids with suction dart guns, mount a target with a challengingly small bull's-eye—and let your kids vie to hit the mark. In case someone actually scores a bull's-eye within the time limit you set, be prepared to hand out a reward of some sort.

CONNECTION

Sin is missing God's target.

Sin Stinks

A couple days before your Bible study, put a large piece of meat in a tightly closed container, let it sit in a warm place, and wait for it to turn rancid. Liver works well.

CONNECTION

When you get to an appropriate place in your lesson on sin, tell them, "Sin stinks." Then open the container and give 'em a whiff. (Yecchhh!)

Velcro Man

Pick up a cheap jumpsuit or something similar at a thrift shop or used clothing store. Then stop by a fabric store and buy twenty feet or so of Velcro tape with self-adhesive backing. Finally, get a hold of a few dozen Ping-Pong balls.

Now tape short Velcro strips (of "hooks") around the Ping-Pong balls, and tape long strips (of "loops") onto the jumpsuit.

You're now ready for a free-for-all intro to the subject of how one's speech and actions affect others.

Assemble your class and ask for a volunteer. Put the kid in the jumpsuit and establish boundaries of movement. Hand out Ping-Pong balls to the rest of the group—and at the signal let them fling away at the jumpsuited target, trying to get the balls to stick.

When the chaos dies down, see how many balls finally ended up sticking. Play this a few times if you want, to determine which "target" has the fewest Ping-Pong balls sticking to her.

CONNECTION

Okay, it's a goofy game—but it's nevertheless an apt illustration of what actually happens in real life. Tell your students,

Every day we say or do things that impact others around us. Much of what we say just bounces off—but sometimes a word, a gesture, an action sticks to a person. If our words and gestures and actions are good and godly, fine. But if they are demeaning or hurtful, they only weigh down a person's heart. Let's take a look at what the Bible has to say about words we carelessly toss around.

Gifted Students

O n a large sheet of paper, list all the spiritual gifts you want to discuss (for starters, see Ephesians 4, 1 Corinthians 12, and Romans 12). Then post a sheet of paper for each person present, with his or her name at the top of the sheet.

Give everyone a marker, with instructions to go to the sheets of people they're familiar with, and—referring as much as necessary to your master list of spiritual gifts—write down at least one gift.

CONNECTION

As a transition into your Bible lesson, you may want to let students explain why they listed certain spiritual gifts. Also point out that everyone in the group has some sort of gift from God that they can use to his glory.

Pass the Baby

A living, squiggling Kickstarter about growing and maturing in Christ.

Arrange for a brave couple to bring their infant to your group. Sit in a circle and pass the infant around—even if it cries or spits up a little.

CONNECTION

Some kids haven't been around infants and won't have the first idea of what to do with one. Yet having simply touched a little baby helps bring the concept of spiritual maturity into better focus. Ask your students,

How would your life change if you had the full responsibility for a baby? In what ways is the treatment of an infant different than a toddler or older kid? What parallels can you draw from a literal baby to a person who would be called a spiritual infant?

Fire in the House!

Students can respond to this Kickstarter in writing (perhaps anonymously) or in a discussion.

Ask your students to imagine that they awoke one night to a fire in their house. If their family and pets were safe and they had the chance to grab only one armful of possessions, what would they take with them?

CONNECTION

People value things differently. Some kids will say they'd scoop up items of cash value—their CD collections, favorite outfits hanging in the closet, and the like. Others will say they'd grab possessions of emotional worth—photos, letters, yearbooks, stuffed animals, trophies, nostalgic gifts.

Say to your students something like—

Why are possessions of emotional worth more valuable to some people than items with a high cash value? Perhaps because, when the heat's on, those people sense what it is that connects them with other people. Plain "stuff" doesn't—even if it's expensive stuff. Let's see what the Bible says about...

And then on to your lesson about material possessions versus "laying up treasures in heaven," or the deceptive appearances of both eternally valuable things as well as merely temporal things, etc.

Blue Smiles

Before students arrive, take a swig of blue or green food coloring. Wash it around in your mouth thoroughly before spitting it out.

As kids arrive, act normal. Talk to them as you usually do. Start the meeting, give announcements, maybe yawn. When students notice your mouth and react, act nonchalant: "Must be something I ate," or "I've been having a little indigestion lately."

CONNECTION

Use your blue smile to illustrate that what we do or how we act speaks louder than what we say. Point out that the youth group was sufficiently distracted by your blue mouth to miss much of what you said. They just couldn't get beyond your blue tongue once they saw it.

Likewise, when Christians explain their faith to others, they had best behave in a way that doesn't neutralize their words.

Planting the Truth in Their Hearts

I ntroduce the concept of growth with a potted plant as well as the elements it needs to grow: a cup of water, a small bag of plant food, light (represented by a flashlight), and air (a balloon).

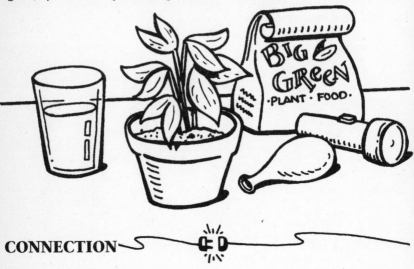

CONNECTION

Say to your students,

Just as a plant needs things like these to flourish, a Christian needs several things to grow spiritually, including Bible study, prayer, fellowship, and confession.

Extend the comparison by discussing pests, insects, and diseases in terms of the problem of sin in a Christian's life.

Goofy Glasses

Head down to a craft store and buy some colored pipe cleaners. There will probably be a big variety of bright colors. Take the pipe cleaners to your meeting and give each student four—from which they all fashion exotic or silly eyeglasses. They must wear their glasses throughout the discussion time.

CONNECTION

Ask them to imagine what they might see if they could slip on a pair of glasses that enabled them to clearly observe the spiritual realm. Are there angelic hosts in the room? What is the spiritual condition of the average human heart? What might they see when somebody dies? What would heaven look like, or hell?

Hard Heart

Get some resin and catalyst (like the two substances that you mix to make epoxy; tell the guys at your hardware store what you want, and they'll steer you to it).

At the meeting pour the resin into a clear cup. Tell the students that the resin will stay fluid (and sticky) indefinitely—until, that is, it is mixed with the catalyst.

Then put a few drops of catalyst into the cup of resin (don't put too much in, or the goop could overheat), and stir it up well. Just for fun, drop a few coins or trinkets into the cup. In just a few minutes, the stuff should begin hardening. By the end of your meeting, it should be hard as rock. (You may want to experiment ahead of time to determine the amount of catalyst you need, so that the mixture sets by the end of your meeting.)

CONNECTION

On your way to your lesson about the effects of sin, say something like—

Unconfessed sin is like the catalyst—once it gets in you, it gradually hardens your heart against God and against others. You can lock up yourself in a prison of bitterness—just like I locked up the coins in the resin. And then only the hammer of Christ's love can crack that hardened heart.

Blank Wall

Tape together large sheets of butcher paper and hang them so that they cover an entire wall of your meeting room. Have lots of markers, too.

As kids come into the room, ask them to grab a pen and create *whatever they like* on the blank wall.

CONNECTION

Some kids will draw or write; some will just hang around and talk with friends. After a few minutes call your group together and point out the results of their opportunity. Say,

Look what you created on your wall! Some of you didn't want to quit when it was time to stop, some of you drew or wrote a little before you lost interest, and some of you never picked up a marker. In a similar way, we have all been given lives—like the blank wall you saw when you walked in—to do something with. You either use your life, or you squander it.

Whoppers

For your Bible study on truthfulness, have 3 x 5 index cards and pencils for everyone. Tell your students to write four statements: three true and one false. They can be statements about themselves, their

families, the world—anything. For example: "I was born in Maine. My mom's middle name is Alberta. My dad served in the Navy. My first parakeet escaped."

When your group is done writing, read each card and have the group vote for which statement they think is the whopper. Award the winners a bag of Whoppers chocolate balls.

CONNECTION

We hear or read whoppers every day—most of them in advertisements, whether on TV, radio, billboards, or in magazines. Yet Christians have a duty to be honest and forthright. Tell your students,

Since truth and integrity are so valuable and so rare, let's look at what the Bible suggests for us as "truth-tellers."

Special Cookie

If your lesson is about our individual uniqueness in Christ, kickstart the lesson this way: bake or buy enough chocolate chip cookies so that each of your students has one. As your kids come into the room, give them a cookie—though with explicit instructions not to eat it, but to *study* it. Carefully. Have them memorize the size, shape, number and arrangement of any visible chocolate pieces or nuts, etc.

Then break into small groups, have each group collect its cookies on a plate—and have everyone in that group try to locate their original cookie (which, if they identify, they can eat). If there is disagreement over whose cookie is whose, let them describe their cookies and advance reasons why their claims are right.

CONNECTION

God has made each of us special and unique. He has given us just the right amount of chips and nuts (so to speak), has made us the right shape and size. We belong to him!

Collage Comment

Bring to the meeting a pile of all kinds of magazines, scissors, a large poster board, and paste. On the poster board write WHAT ARE THEY REALLY SELLING?

Ask your students to dig through the magazines for examples of ads that use something besides the product to sell the product (sex or prestige to sell cars, healthy-looking families to sell cereal, etc.). Students should cut out the ad and paste it on the board, with a caption that says what's *really* being sold.

CONNECTION

God deals in truth. He doesn't try to snow us. Ask your students,

On a scale of 1 to 10 (1 being obvious and insulting, 10 being smooth and convincing), how would you rate the level of trickery used in these ads? Do you think that Jesus used any sales techniques to communicate his truth? If so, what?

Time Line

On a long piece of butcher paper posted on the wall, draw a time line whose first year is just prior to the birth of your students and the final year is a hundred years from now. As kids come in, hand out markers. Ask everyone to mark on the time line when they think major events of their lives will take place: college graduation, first new car, first "real" job, marriage, children, death. Your kids should write their names by each of their entries.

Compare what various kids have written. Ask them for comments or reasons for marking the time line the way they did.

Incidentally, if you're around for the marriage or parenthood of any of your students—or for a youth group reunion a decade from now—this butcher-paper time line can become meaningful to students.

CONNECTION

Each of us has only one life. What we do with it depends on our use of time and on God's grace in giving us years. Use this time line as an introduction to the topic of using our time wisely. Tell your students,

We live on a continuum that progresses forward in time. We cannot relive the past, we cannot visit the future. The present is God's gift to us—we are what we are in the present. Today let's consider how we can use what time we have wisely.

Slightly Misspoken

R ead these statements to your group. Ask your students if they have any idea of the speaker or at least the setting of the statements.

• "Come, come! Why, they couldn't hit an elephant at this dist—" *(Union Major General John Sedgwick, shot dead as he looked over a bunker at the Confederate Army during the battle of Spotsylvania)*

• "I'm so healthy I expect to live on and on." *(nutritionist and organic farmer J. I. Rodale to talk-show host Dick Cavett while taping a TV show, just moments before he dropped dead of a heart attack)*

• "I cannot imagine any condition which would cause the ship to founder. I cannot conceive of any vital disaster happening to this vessel. Modern shipbuilding has gone beyond that." *(Edward J. Smith, captain of the* Titanic*)*

• "Take it easy driving. The life you save may be mine." *(actor James Dean, spoken in a public-service message two weeks before he was killed while speeding in his Porsche)*

• "I could whip all the Indians on the continent with the Seventh Cavalry." *(General George Armstrong Custer)*

CONNECTION

These statements—and the events that soon followed them—underline the fact that we simply can't control our environment like we want to. We can't even evaluate our own strengths and weaknesses accurately. God is the only one qualified to be followed and depended upon with unshaken trust.

Ask your students,

What do these last words tell you about the ideas or thoughts of the speakers? Obviously, what they believed didn't match the reality they were actually in. Let's take a look at why we shouldn't take our own wisdom too seriously—and why we should take God's wisdom *very* seriously.

Tricky Cookies

Teaching about the need to see through sheep's clothing to the wolves underneath? Replace some of the cream-filled cookies in a bag of Oreos with fraudulent ones—Oreos in which the cream has been replaced with white toothpaste.

Munch on a real Oreo while you pass the bag around. Some of the kids will wolf down the fakes, giving you a fun intro into your lesson.

CONNECTION

Tell your students,

Okay, okay—that <u>was</u> a dirty trick. But Satan has plenty of dirty tricks up his sleeve. Today let's talk about some of the ways he fools us and how we can protect ourselves with God's help.

Guess the Slogan

Your students are to guess a famous advertising slogan. Explain that you will give them the slogan one word at a time until someone guesses it correctly. Warm them up with Nike's easy motto: "Just—" and they will quickly finish, "—do it." For the real McCoy, give them, one word at a time, "Fly the Friendly Skies of United." See how few words the group needs to guess the entire slogan.

CONNECTION

Just as well-known slogans and logos represent specific companies and products, so Jesus is the Word of God—he represents the Father to us.

Cotton Candy Thinking

H owever you define "worldly thinking" for your group, this Kickstarter will get you going down the right path.

On your way to the meeting, stop by a candy store for a bag of cotton candy. (You'd better pick up some Wet Wipes, too, for sticky hands.) At the meeting pull a handful of cotton candy out of the bag and pass it around so all can have some—while you list its selling points: sweet taste, pretty color, looks great, you can get a lot for your money, fun to eat, etc. Then list what you get in cotton candy—not much. All show and little substance. (Example: it may look like a bag full, but compare its weight with that of a couple Snickers bars.)

CONNECTION

A lot of what passes for smarts in this world is really only cotton candy for the mind—pretty and pink and sweet, but hardly worth what you'll pay for it. Ask your kids the following questions:

- *What makes cotton candy a desirable object worth paying money for?*
- *As a candy, do you think cotton candy is as good a deal as other candies? Why or why not?*
- *Anything disappointing about cotton candy?*
- *Can you think of something that might be considered cotton candy for the mind?*
- *What are some similarities between cotton candy and the ideas of the world?*

What Are the Odds?

Use these statistics as a jumping-off point for a Bible study on worry. Ask your students to guess the odds for the following situations. Toss a small prize to the kid who comes the closest to the correct odds for each statistic.

1. The odds of dying in a plane crash: *1 in 400,000*
2. The odds of a frequent motorcycle rider to be in a fatal accident this year: *1 in 1,000*
3. The odds of you dying by being hit by a meteor this year: *1 in 5 billion*
4. The odds of you dying by the bite of a snake, spider, or any poisonous beastie this year: *1 in 21 million*
5. The lifetime odds of you dying of AIDS: *1 in 97*
6. The odds of you being injured by a twister this year: *1 in 200,000*
7. The odds of you being hit by lighting during your lifetime: *1 in 9,000*
8. The odds that you will get heartburn today: *1 in 150*
9. The odds that you are color-blind: *1 in 100*
10. The odds that you will injure yourself while shaving, seriously enough to get medical attention: *1 in 7,000*
11. The odds that you will eventually die: *1 in 1*

CONNECTION

Tell your students,

A lot of people worry about things that will never really harm them—and this easily results in neglecting things that need their attention. Learning when to trust God and where to invest our concern is what we need to discover.

Wearin' the Wealth

To give your teenagers an inkling of how well off they are in this country, have them total up how much was probably paid for everything they are wearing, including accessories like wallets, watches,

and jewelry. Start with yourself as an example—calculate your "worth" on a chalkboard or overhead projector.

Even casually dressed teenagers are likely to be wearing $100 or more in value. Mention that the average income in many third-world nations is less than $400—*annually*. Well-dressed Westerners walk around with more wealth on their bodies than many people earn in a year.

CONNECTION

Transition into your lesson about what Jesus taught about wealth, sharing what we have with others, etc.

The Not-Quite-Easiest Quiz in the World

Photocopy the quiz questions on page 111 and give a copy to each of your students (or photocopy or hand write the questions onto an overhead transparency—or simply read the questions aloud). After students hazard their guesses to each question, give the answer and award one point for each correct answer. Give a prize to the kid who gets the most correct answers.

Here are the questions and answers:

1. How long did the 100 Years War last? *116 years (from 1337 to 1453)*
2. Which country makes Panama hats? *Ecuador*
3. From which animals do we get catgut? *sheep and horses*
4. In which month do Russians celebrate the October Revolution? *November (the Russian calendar was 13 days behind ours)*
5. What is a camel's hair brush made of? *squirrel fur*
6. The Canary Islands in the Pacific are named after what animal? *dogs (the Latin name for the islands is* Insularia Canaria, *Island of the Dogs)*
7. What was King George VI's first name? *Albert (when he came to the throne in 1936, he respected the wish of Queen Victoria that no future king should ever be called Albert)*
8. What color is a purple finch? *distinctively crimson*
9. Where are Chinese gooseberries from? *New Zealand*
10. How long did the 30 Years War last? *30 years, of course (from 1618 to 1648)*

CONNECTION

Questions like these are a great reminder that our best logic can be dead wrong. Tell your students,

This little quiz demonstrates how easy it is to think we have the right answer when we don't. We're all fallible and, despite our best efforts, we often fail to make the right decisions. God, on the other hand, sees and understands things that we don't. You can trust his foresight and his plans for you.

The Not-Quite-Easiest Quiz in the World

1. How long did the 100 Years War last?

2. Which country makes Panama hats?

3. From which animals do we get catgut?

4. In which month do Russians celebrate the October Revolution?

5. What is a camel's hair brush made of?

6. The Canary Islands in the Pacific are named after what animal?

7. What was King George VI's first name?

8. What color is a purple finch?

9. Where are Chinese gooseberries from?

10. How long did the 30 Years War last?

Isn't This a Face You Can Trust?

You need to trust God even when it's tempting not to—that's what this little game demonstrates.

Before the meeting prepare a number of bite-sized goodies—pieces of candy, slices of fruit, etc. Also prepare and seal in Tupperware containers a few foul-smelling items spread onto popsicle sticks—Limburger cheese, sour milk, and so on. Get a few blindfolds and you are ready to go.

To begin your study, select three or four student volunteers. Tell them, "I need some help with a project. Would you trust me if I told you that I would never do anything that would make you ill or harm you in any way?" If they say yes—which you hope they will—send them out of the room.

When they're gone, tell the audience that when the volunteers come back into the room blindfolded, and are just about to taste what you will feed them, they are to yell, "No! Don't eat it! Oh gross!" and similar exclamations.

Bring the volunteers back in one at a time, blindfolded. Sit the victim in a chair and say, "I'm going to give you something that is delicious to eat. No matter what you hear being said or what you might sense going on around you, trust me."

Ask your victim to stick out his tongue. Even as an assistant slides the popsicle stick with a foul smell under the person's nose, you spoon into his mouth chocolate pudding or something similarly delicious. See who actually allows you to put food in their mouth and eats it.

CONNECTION

God has been known to ask us to trust him, even when our senses—or other people—tell us to trust ourselves. But God will never steer us wrong.

Cleaning Up
Your Act

Take a look at the hundreds of cleaning products where you shop. You'll find Joy, Glad, Mr. Clean...ever notice the Christian sound many of these brand names have?

So plan a message around the names of such products! You can throw in more than just cleaning products—*Time* magazine, Sure deodorant, Armor-All vinyl protector.

Say you're teaching on the armor of God (Ephesians 6). Start by mentioning that educators have demonstrated that visual aids cause students to remember a lesson much better than merely listening to words. Then proceed into your spiel: each time you use the name of a product in a sentence, hold up the product.

> If you want joy *(hold up the soap)* in your life *(hold up the cereal)*, remember that the Bible says to wear your spiritual armor all *(hold up the Armor-All)* the time *(hold up the magazine)*.

Write yourself a short, five-minute script (it's really not that hard), and you'll have your audience rolling. (Sure, you'll drop some bucks on products, but either the church custodial closet or the cabinet under your bathroom sink at home will be stocked for a year.)

CONNECTION

Put all the products off to one side, then swing into your message.

Covered with Labels

Kickstart a lesson on the fallacies of stereotyping people with labels (stupid, nerd, ugly, etc.) by sticking large self-adhesive labels all over your own clothes and face. Your students can suggest stereotypes to write on the labels.

CONNECTION

Tell your students something like this:

In this world we all seem to be slapped with labels we must wear. Yet as we trust God and live the way he wants us to, we become better people. God helps us tear many of those labels off.

Toe Sucker

Come with ten bucks (in one-dollar bills)—and be prepared to part with it.

Start a discussion with your group about what people are willing to do for money. For example, for enough money most high schoolers would walk naked through school at lunch time. (You might want to show a relevant clip from the old film *The Magic Christian*, in which nattily dressed British businessmen plunge into a cesspool to retrieve cash that had been dumped into it.)

Some kids will be honest enough to admit the price at which they can be bought. Others may hold out, denying the possibility outright.

Tell your group that money has power to make normally decent people do what they typically wouldn't—and that you'll demonstrate this truth. Then offer cash to anyone who will momentarily suck (or lick or kiss) your big toe. Start with a dollar, and keep raising the amount until you get a taker. Chances are, someone will be willing to trade their dignity for some cash by the time you reach ten bucks.

Make a big production of peeling off your shoe and sock and of the toe suck itself. Most kids will be grossed out.

CONNECTION

Tell your students,

You can see for yourself that money can motivate people to do some pretty gross stuff. You can also see that, if my price kept going up, most of you would be sucking on my toe, too. Now let's look at money and its ability to motivate us.

Last Word

To kickstart a lesson about living a meaningful life, start with some humorous words about death. Read these actual epitaphs to your group, or post them.

- John Edwards, who perished in a fire 1904—No one could hold a candle to him.
- Bunn—Here Lies John Bunn Who was killed by a gun. His name wasn't Bunn; his real name was Wood, But Wood wouldn't rhyme with gun, So I thought Bunn should.
- Strange—Here Lies an Honest Lawyer—That is Strange.
- Maggie (a U.S. Army mule buried in France)—In memory of MAGGIE Who in her time kicked Two Colonels Four Majors Ten Captains Twenty-Four Lieutenants, Forty-Two sergeants, Four hundred and thirty-two other ranks AND One Mills Bomb.
- Lowder—Here lies the remains of Mary Ann Lowder She burst while drinking a seltzer powder. Called from the world to her heavenly rest, She should have waited 'till it effervesced.

Now ask your students to create an epitaph—serious or humorous, your call—for another person in the group. Read them aloud when everyone's finished.

CONNECTION

Tell your group,

An epitaph can sum up what the deceased person valued or contributed in life. Most of us would like to think that our lives mean something, that they have value and purpose. Yet much of what humans spend their time and energy on has no lasting value. Let's look at the kind of life that has purpose, that lasts a lifetime—and beyond.

Youth Specialties Titles

Professional Resources
Developing Spiritual Growth in Junior High Students
Developing Student Leaders
Equipped to Serve: Volunteer Youth Worker Training Course
Help! I'm a Junior High Youth Worker!
Help! I'm a Sunday School Teacher!
Help! I'm a Volunteer Youth Worker!
How to Expand Your Youth Ministry
How to Recruit and Train Volunteer Youth Workers
How to Speak to Youth...and Keep Them Awake at the Same Time
One Kid at a Time: Reaching Youth through Mentoring
Peer Counseling in Youth Groups
Advanced Peer Counseling in Youth Groups
A Youth Ministry Crash Course

Discussion Starter Resources
Get 'Em Talking
4th-6th Grade TalkSheets
High School TalkSheets
Junior High TalkSheets
High School TalkSheets: Psalms and Proverbs
Junior High TalkSheets: Psalms and Proverbs
More High School TalkSheets
More Junior High TalkSheets
Parent Ministry TalkSheets
What If...? 450 Thought-Provoking Questions to Get Teenagers Talking, Laughing, and
    Thinking
Would You Rather...? 465 Provocative Questions to Get Teenagers Talking

Ideas Library
Combos: 1-4, 5-8, 9-12, 13-16, 17-20, 21-24, 25-28, 29-32, 33-36, 37-40, 41-44, 45-48,
    49-52, 53-56
Ideas Index

Youth Ministry Programming
Compassionate Kids: Practical Ways to Involve Your Students in Mission and Service
Creative Bible Lessons in John: Encounters with Jesus
Creative Bible Lessons in Romans: Faith on Fire!
Creative Bible Lessons on the Life of Christ
Creative Junior High Programs from A to Z, Vol. 1 (A-M)
Creative Programming Ideas for Junior High Ministry
Dramatic Pauses
Facing Your Future: Graduating Youth Group with a Faith That Lasts
Great Fundraising Ideas for Youth Groups
More Great Fundraising Ideas for Youth Groups

(continued next page)

Youth Specialties Titles (continued)

Great Retreats for Youth Groups
Greatest Skits on Earth
Greatest Skits on Earth, Vol. 2
Hot Illustrations for Youth Talks
More Hot Illustrations for Youth Talks
Kickstarters: 101 Ingenious Intros to Just About Any Bible Lesson
Memory Makers
Hot Talks
Incredible Questionnaires for Youth Ministry
Junior High Game Nights
More Junior High Game Nights
Play It! Great Games for Groups
Play It Again! More Great Games for Groups
Road Trip
Spontaneous Melodramas
Super Sketches for Youth Ministry
Teaching the Bible Creatively
Up Close and Personal: How to Build Community in Your Youth Group
Wild Truth Bible Lessons
Worship Services for Youth Groups

Clip Art
ArtSource Vol. 1—Fantastic Activities
ArtSource Vol. 2—Borders, Symbols, Holidays, and Attention Getters
ArtSource Vol. 3—Sports
ArtSource Vol. 4—Phrases and Verses
ArtSource Vol. 5—Amazing Oddities and Appalling Images
ArtSource Vol. 6—Spiritual Topics
ArtSource Vol. 7—Variety Pack

Videos
Edge TV
The Heart of Youth Ministry: A Morning with Mike Yaconelli
Next Time I Fall in Love Video Curriculum
Promo Spots for Junior High Game Nights
Understanding Your Teenager Video Curriculum

Student Books
Grow For It Journal
Grow For It Journal through the Scriptures
Wild Truth Journal for Junior Highers